Date Due

DISCARDED

SEP 0 3 2008

BRODART, CO.   Cat. No. 23-233-003   Printed in U.S.A.

Getting Started

Materials and Equipment for Active Learning Preschools

Nancy Vogel

HIGH/SCOPE PRESS

Ypsilanti, Michigan

Published by
High/Scope® Press

A Division of the
High/Scope Educational Research Foundation
600 North River Street
Ypsilanti, Michigan 48198-2898
(313) 485-2000, FAX (313) 485-0704

Nancy Altman Brickman, High/Scope Press Editor
Cathy Doran-McMillion, Cover and Text Design
Gregory Fox, Photography

Library of Congress Cataloging-in-Publication Data

Vogel, Nancy, 1970–
        Getting Started : materials and equipment for active learning preschools /
        Nancy Vogel.
            p.   cm.
        Includes bibliographical references.
        ISBN 1-57379-055-9
        1. Education, Preschool—Equipment and supplies. 2. Teaching—Aids and
devices. 3. Active learning—Equipment and supplies.
I. Title.
LB1140.3.V64   1997   97-16593
372.133—dc21   CIP

Printed in the United States of America

Contents

Introduction *1*

*T*his book is for you—an adult who is working with young children in a High/Scope active learning classroom or center. The suggestions given in the pages that follow are intended to help you select materials and equipment that will support children's cognitive, physical, and social development. Whether you are planning an entirely new High/Scope setting or making changes in an existing setting, this guide is designed to assist your planning process.

Most of this guide consists of comprehensive lists of equipment and materials for specific "interest areas" in High/Scope classrooms. Before turning to these specific recommendations, however, the book briefly summarizes some basic principles for arranging High/Scope learning environments. Following this discussion and the lists of materials, the book concludes with diagrams of three sample room arrangements.

Guidelines for Arranging the Classroom

So, let's get started! To understand the lists of suggested materials in the book, you'll need some background on High/Scope principles for arranging the early childhood classroom or center. These principles are discussed fully in the High/Scope preschool manual *Educating Young Children: Active Learning Practices for Preschool and Child Care Programs,* by Mary Hohmann and David P. Weikart, High/Scope Press, 1995. (See especially Chapter 5, "Arranging and Equipping Spaces

Some interest areas are planned for multiple uses. This block area is spacious enough to accommodate music and movement activities.

for Active Learning.") Briefly summarized, here are some key guidelines for arranging High/Scope learning environments:

✔ **Divide the space into well-defined interest areas for distinctive types of play and stock each interest area with a wide range of stimulating materials.** Four basic interest areas—the art, block, house, and toy areas—are included in all High/Scope settings. In this guide these four basic areas are discussed first. Space for books, the fifth area discussed in this book, is also an essential part of every High/Scope classroom. However, this space is not always treated as a separate interest area; in smaller classrooms, it may be necessary to incorporate the reading space into another interest area, such as the house or toy area. Various other interest areas may be developed by staff of individual High/Scope programs to reflect the needs, interests, and cultures of children and program staff. In this guide the following additional interest areas are discussed: computers, music and movement, sand and water, and woodworking. These are just a few of the many possible interest areas that can be temporary or permanent parts of High/Scope settings.

✔ **Choose names for the interest areas that children can understand.** Use terms that make sense to children, for example, "toy area" instead of "manipulative area," "house area" instead of "dramatic play area."

✔ **Establish visual boundaries.** For example, spaces may be defined by low shelves, floor coverings, boxes, storage containers, even easels and tables.

✔ **In developing a floor plan, consider the fixed elements of the physical setting (sinks, toilets, floor surfaces, doors, and electrical outlets) and the traffic flow within and between the interest areas.** Consider the activities that occur in each area, and the physical features needed for those activities. For example, locate the art area near a sink and on a tile floor. Consider also how children's activities in one area may affect those in nearby areas. For example, house area play often spills into the block area, so locate these areas next to or near each other. Similarly, locate areas for relatively quiet activities next to each other (book area next to toy or computer area).

✔ **Plan the interest areas to accommodate many types of play.** Include spaces where children can pretend, build things, explore materials, and use the large and small muscles. In each interest area, include spaces where children can play alone, side by side, or in small groups.

✔ **Modify the interest areas throughout the year.** Depending on children's interests, shift and add to the materials and interest areas as the year progresses. Consider introducing new materials during a small-group activity, then include the children in the process of deciding where and how to store the new items.

✔ **Choose materials that reflect the children's interests.** Observe the children to see what they play with during the day, and add new materials to the interest areas that may extend their play.

✔ **Choose materials that are appropriate for the children's developmental levels and that support the following types of play typical of young children:**

- **Exploratory play—exploring the properties and functions of materials:** string, glue, tape, Play-Doh, water, dried beans, musical instruments, and other materials with interesting properties or functions.

- **Constructive play—making and building:** blocks, art materials, wood scraps, cardboard tubes, carpet scraps, and so forth.

- **Dramatic play—pretending:** dress-up clothes and related props, for example, hair dryer, blender, office supplies, restaurant supplies, luggage, kitchen equipment.

- **Games—exploring and playing simple games with rules:** cards, dice, beans, counters, pads of paper, and other materials for playing made-up games or simple conventional games.

✔ **Provide items that can be used in a variety of ways.** Choose "open-ended" materials. These are materials that can be used in an infinite number of ways by children and accommodate easily to children's different interests and developmental needs.

✔ **Choose materials that reflect the experiences and cultures of the children in the program, and that reflect human diversity in unbiased ways.** Bring the interests and cultures of the children into the classroom by building on the direct experiences of the children. This can be accomplished by carefully observing the children you work with, viewing parents as team members who can serve as volunteers and resources, encouraging children to share information about their families, and planning field trips to the immediate community and neighborhood. Through such efforts, you can learn about the foods, home languages, leisure-time activities, celebrations, music, clothing, and occupations of children's family members, and you can add materials to the classroom that reflect these and other aspects of children's family and community experiences. Choose materials that will reaffirm children's identities as well as those that help them learn about other people and the connections between these lives and their own. Provide books, dolls, toy figures, puzzles, and so forth that depict a variety of racial, ethnic, and cultural groups and that avoid sex-role stereotyping.

Storage shelves are labeled with pictures or outlines of the materials.

✔ **Make sure the materials are safe, clean, and well maintained.** Always consider safety when ordering materials and equipment for your classroom. Beware of shelving units or other pieces of equipment that may be too high, possibly obstructing your view of the children or tipping over. If you have equipment like this, you might consider putting it against a wall, and using other pieces of equipment to define your interest areas. If the children in your class tend to put materials in their mouths, choose items that are larger to avoid possible choking. Toys, equipment, and other materials should be cleaned, disinfected, and inspected regularly for damage or dangerous pieces or edges. Replace or repair damaged materials.

✔ **Store materials so that children can reach them.** Store materials on low, open shelving, in sturdy containers, on the floor, or in other locations easily accessible to children.

✔ **Label shelves and containers so that children can find and put away materials.** Both the container and the shelf where the container goes should be labeled with the identical label. Use labels that children can "read," for example, pieces of the material itself, tracings, drawings, catalog pictures, box tops, photographs, or photocopies. Occasionally include the word for the item along with a label that can be visually understood.

✔ **Use see-through containers to store materials in plain view.** Clear plastic containers work best for storage because children can see through them, but baskets and other types of canisters work well, too.

✔ **Make sure materials are consistently stored in the same place so that children know where to find them.**

The guidelines listed above should be helpful to you in arranging and planning your classroom both initially and throughout the school year. The next section provides background information on another key element of the High/Scope framework, the daily routine.

Elements of the High/Scope Daily Routine

As you read, you will notice that reference is made to various parts of the High/Scope daily routine. While each preschool or center organizes its schedule to meet the needs of the children and families it serves, a High/Scope daily routine in any setting is created from the same basic "building blocks." These basic daily routine segments are described below. These elements can occur in any order, with the exception of the sequence of planning time, work time, cleanup time, and recall time. These four elements always occur in the same order without being interrupted by other parts of the routine.

The basic High/Scope daily routine elements are as follows:

• **Greeting time (15–20 minutes).** Greeting time occurs at the beginning of the day or early in the day. Greeting time provides a smooth transition from home to school and gives children and adults a chance to share important information for the day and to read and explore books together.

- **Planning time (10 minutes).** Children indicate what they choose to do during work time (typically what they will do first). Adults help children articulate their plans and often try to help children extend their plans.

- **Work time (45 minutes–1 hour).** Children carry out their initial and subsequent plans. Children can work with any of the materials in any of the interest areas. Adults observe children and look for opportunities to enter into children's activities. As they work with children, adults encourage their thinking, extend their play, and support them in solving problems.

- **Cleanup time (10 minutes).** Children and adults together return materials and equipment to their storage spaces and, when appropriate, put away or find display space for their personal creations.

- **Recall time (10 minutes).** Recall brings closure to the sequence of planning, working, and recalling. Children reflect on, talk about, and/or show what they have done at work time.

- **Snack or meal times (20 minutes).** Children and adults share nutritious food and interesting conversation together in a relaxed, family-like setting.

- **Large-group time (15–20 minutes).** Children and adults get together to play games, tell and re-enact stories, sing songs, do fingerplays, dance, play musical instruments, or reenact special events. This time is an opportunity for each child to participate in a large group, sharing ideas and learning from the ideas of others, as well as a time for adults to introduce new learning opportunities.

- **Small-group time (15–20 minutes).** Each adult meets with a consistent small group of children (about six to ten children) to work with materials planned and introduced by the adult. Although the adult chooses and introduces the materials, each child has control over what he or she will do with these materials.

- **Outside time (30 minutes).** Children engage in vigorous, noisy outdoor play. Adults participate in and support children's play in the outdoor setting.

- **Adults' daily team planning (20–30 minutes).** Classroom adults meet together to discuss what they observed and learned about individual children during that day's session. They share and record anecdotes, and they plan for the next day's activities based on what children were doing that day.

How This Book Is Organized

You will notice that this book is organized by sections corresponding to the interest areas that are commonly found in a High/Scope classroom. Included in each section is a brief explanation of the interest area, including suggestions for locating it within the classroom and various ideas for displaying the materials found in the area. After each description, there is a list of

When materials are stored in consistent locations, children learn to get them out and put them away independently.

the equipment needed, and finally a detailed list of materials suggested for the area. Following the sections on each interest area, we have included sample room arrangements of classrooms, both large and small, with accompanying rationales. These are intended to give you a more concrete picture of possible classroom designs.

This book can be used to assist a teacher or director in equipping a first-year classroom or in adding materials to a classroom that has been in operation for several years. The lists of materials are headed by the terms "first year," and "later years." These recommended time frames are meant as flexible guidelines that the staff of individual programs must adapt to their particular situations. For example, the equipment and materials listed for the first year may be items that a program in its beginning stages may work toward acquiring. While some new programs may be able to purchase these materials almost immediately, for other programs this may take several years. The equipment and materials found under the "later years" heading may be items that a program may wish to add after accumulating most of the items from the "first year" list. Remember, these lists were created with the ideal active learning classroom in mind, and it may take your program some time to obtain all of the materials suggested. Also, depending on your budget requirements, the interests of children in your program, and other factors, you may want to prioritize, in a more detailed way, the purchases you plan with these lists. As the lists stand now, the headings "first year" and "later years" provide only a general time frame for acquiring materials and equipment. You may wish to rank the items in the lists according to their importance for your program and then set up a more specific timetable for acquiring them.

Appropriate Materials for Young Children

In setting up an active learning environment, it is important to stock your classroom with a plentiful supply of the types of materials that are interesting to young children. The lists of materials in this booklet emphasize the following *general* types of materials that are appropriate for and appealing to young children:

- **Practical everyday objects**—objects that children see parents and other important people using, such as real pots and pans, purses, tires, staplers, pencils, pens, markers, and paper.

- **Natural and found materials**—objects such as pine cones, acorns, shells, and leaves are considered "natural" materials. "Found" materials consist of used or scrap manufactured materials available free or at a low cost, such as wallpaper scraps, plywood scraps, bottle caps, and empty margarine tubs.

- **Tools**—objects that help to "get the job done," such as shovels, brooms, buckets, sponges, hammers, and saws.

- **Messy materials**—materials that are interesting to touch, such as shaving cream, paint, sand, water, paste, and dough.

- **Heavy, large materials**—objects that require children to use their whole bodies and large muscles while manipulating them. Examples include hollow blocks, boxes, tricycles, balls, tree stump slices, and other objects to climb on.

- **Easy-to-handle materials**—objects that fit easily into children's hands, such as buttons, pegs and pegboards, beads, bean bags, maracas, and tambourines.

Note that the above list includes many inexpensive or free materials that are typically collected rather than purchased. These recycled and found items appeal to children because they can be used for so many different purposes. Examples of such materials include office and computer paper with one blank side, junk mail, fabric scraps, paper-towel tubes, egg cartons, bottle caps, paper scraps, packing peanuts, dress-up clothes, kitchen equipment, and small used appliances with the cords cut off. Creating a list of recyclable materials and household objects that are needed and sending the list home to the parents in your classroom is one way of collecting such materials. In some areas there are organizations that collect recyclable and scrap materials donated by local companies. These organizations then sell these materials (at low cost) to educational and recreational programs or individuals. If organizations like these are not found in your community, you can purchase scrap materials directly from the High/Scope Educational Research Foundation (look for Scrap Box materials in the High/Scope Press catalog or call 1-800-40-PRESS).

At High/Scope, we understand that each program has a unique group of

High/Scope classrooms are stocked with many open-ended materials—such as paper and tape—that children can use in their own inventive ways.

children with unique interests, and that room sizes, budgets, class sizes, and so forth vary from program to program. The bottom line is that no two groups are the same. However, for the purposes of this book we used an average class size of 20 children to estimate the quantities of materials needed for each area of the classroom. You will note that the recommended quantity for a given material or tool is often 12. In such cases, we estimated with small-group time in mind. A quantity of 12 allows for one item per child in a small group of 10 children, plus two extra items to keep on hand. Depending on your class size and the size of your small groups, you may wish to adjust these numbers when equipping your classroom. Note, too, that many of the items listed are consumables that have to be replenished on a regular basis. The quantities given are intended to last a year, but obviously there may be wide variations in how quickly supplies are depleted. Program staff must check their supplies frequently to avoid running out of materials and to keep tabs on which materials are interesting to children.

2

The Art Area

A High/Scope art area is typically filled with busy, curious children who are drawing, painting, making models, cutting, pasting, taping, and stapling. As they work with other children or with adults, these children are carrying out their plans and making new plans. Children in the art area are usually eager to explore and create with a variety of materials. As with other areas in a High/Scope classroom, it is essential that the art area has a wide enough variety of materials to satisfy children's interests. It is also important to provide enough of each material or tool so that more than one child at a time can work with an item. As you choose materials for the art area, be aware of children's need to represent a wide variety of people, especially those that look like their family members and people in the community. For example, crayons that reflect the actual skin tones of various ethnic groups are now available. Also remember to have materials available so that children can try out the arts and crafts typical of the local community (for example, supplies for weaving, clay work, or sewing).

Locate the art area near the classroom's water source to allow children to use water for mixing paints and cleaning up. Easily cleaned tile or vinyl flooring is best for the art area, but if this is not available, cover the floor with plastic drop cloths, shower curtains, or newspapers. The table in the art area (which is usually also used during small-group and snack times) should be large enough to accommodate an adult and 10 children. When designing the art area, set aside space for drying and displaying children's artwork. Low drying racks and bulletin boards allow children to put away or hang up their own art projects, rather than depend on adults for assistance.

Shelving units in the art area should allow enough space for displaying all of the different types of materials. A unit with numerous narrow shelves at the top and several "cubby holes" at the bottom allows for the convenient storage of colored construction paper, as well as materials such as staplers, glue, tape, and envelopes. Additional shelving units may hold Play-Doh, rolling pins, cotton balls, empty toilet paper rolls, lids from bottles, and toothpicks, and a wide range of other purchased and found materials.

This marker holder gives children ready access to the markers and prevents the caps from getting lost.

Art Area Equipment

First Year

Double easel
Drying rack
Sectioned shelving unit,*
  48"l x 34"h x 13"d

Shelving unit,* 48"l x 30"h x 13"d
Table (large enough to seat 10
  children plus 1 teacher)
Chairs (11)

Later Years

Additional shelving unit,*
  48"l x 30"h x 13"d

Additional double easel
  (if space allows)

Art Area Materials

First Year

Liquid tempera paint (1-gal. con-
  tainer each color): black,
  blue, brown, green, red, orange,
  violet, white, yellow
Washable finger paint (1-qt. con-
  tainer each color): red, yellow, blue
Washable watercolor paint sets (12)
Paint cups with lids (24)
Paintbrushes, long handle,
  1" width (24)
Paintbrushes, short handle,
  1/2" width (24)
Sponges, for sponge painting (48)
Vinyl smocks (12, may be shared
  with sand and water area)
Shaving cream (5 cans)
Food coloring
Scissors (12)
Scissor holder
Glue bottles, 4-oz. size (12)
Glue, for refilling glue
  bottles (2 gal.)
Masking tape (24 rolls)
Tape dispensers (12)
Clear tape (24 rolls)
Staplers (12)
Staples (5 boxes)
Paper punches (12)

Paper clips, jumbo (5 boxes)
Rubber bands (5 boxes)
String
Yarn
Play-Doh, various colors
  (24 containers, 6 oz. each, or
  equivalent quantity homemade)
Rolling pins (12)
Cookie cutters (48)
Pencils, regular-sized (4 boxes)
Pencil sharpeners, small (6)
Colored pencils, (4 boxes)
Markers, classic colors (24 boxes)
Markers, flesh tones (4 boxes)
Marker holders (2)
Crayons (24 boxes)
Crayons, flesh tones (4 boxes)
Chalk (2 boxes)
Sidewalk chalk (2 buckets)
Ink pads (12)
Ink pad stamps (48)
Magazines
Catalogs
Construction paper
  (5 packages each color): black,
  blue, brown, green, red, orange,
  violet, white, yellow, pink, light
  blue, gray
White drawing paper (10 packages)

* Dimensions of shelving may vary depending on brand selected.

Newsprint, for easel,
(2 packages, each 500 sheets)
Paper scraps ,
White paper, 36" width,
(1 roll—1000')
Paper plates (100)
Shoe boxes
Wallpaper scraps and
old sample books

Cardboard scraps
Wooden, plastic, or homemade
stencils (1 set upper-case alphabet,
1 set lower-case alphabet, 24
shapes)
Stationery/cards, used
Stamps/stickers
Coffee filters (1 box)
Additional found materials

Later Years

Washable finger paints (1-qt. container each color): black, brown,
green, orange, violet, white
Squeeze bottles (12)
Paint bowls (24)
Soap flakes
Eyedroppers (36)
Toothbrushes (36)
Craft scissors,
with serrated blades (12)
Glue sticks (12)
Craft shape paper punches (24)
Clay

Clay presses or garlic presses (12)
Clay hammers (12)
Clay-modeling tools (12)
Small chalkboards (12)
Dry-erase markers (36)
Small dry-erase boards (12)
Craft tissue paper, assorted colors
(2 packages, 100 sheets each)
Powder tempera paint (1-qt. container each color): red,
yellow, blue
Spray bottles (12)

Children take care of hanging up their own projects when a drying rack is conveniently located.

*F*or more information on arranging and equipping the art area, see *Educating Young Children: Active Learning Practices for Preschool and Child Care Programs,* by Mary Hohmann and David P. Weikart, High/Scope Press, 1995, pp. 132–135.

3

The Block Area

*I*n the block area children work and play alone or together building roads, castles, houses, zoos, hospitals, and farms. They use various sizes of blocks (ranging from small unit blocks to large hollow blocks) and many types of props (toy cars, trucks, trains, animals, barns).

Block area play is often active and social. The block area must be large enough to accommodate small groups of children playing actively, as well as the large structures, roads, and other creations children make there. In addition, in most High/Scope classrooms, the block area also serves as the meeting place for large-group time and thus must be large enough to accommodate the whole group. Because

Since block area play is often highly social, you'll need plenty of room to accommodate groupings of children.

Children often use dress-up materials, such as these fireman hats, in their block area play.

this area lends itself to dramatic play, it makes sense to position it near the house area so that children playing in the block area can use the house area's dress-up clothes, kitchen items, and other props. To reduce noise and increase comfort, cover the block area floor with carpet or a large area rug.

This area's blocks and props require plenty of shelving space. Unit blocks can be placed directly on an appropriately labeled, divided shelving unit, while the large hollow blocks may be stored on labels taped to the floor. Props such as cars and animals are kept in labeled storage containers and stored on low shelves that are clearly labeled. Note that some small building toys, such as Lincoln Logs or Tinkertoys, may be located either in the block or toy area.

Shelves define the boundaries of the block area as well as provide well-organized storage for block area materials.

Block Area Equipment

First Year

Shelving units, 48"l x 30"h x 13"d (2)

Later Years

Shelving units, 48"l x 30"h x 13"d (2)

Block Area Materials

First Year

Unit blocks,* ordered individually:
  Half units (10)
  Basic units (20)
  Double units (10)
  Quad units (4)
  Ramps (4)
  Unit arches (4)
  Half circles (2)
  Small half circles (4)
  Half Roman arches (4)
  Small buttresses (4)
  Quarter-circle arches (4)
  Half-circle arches (2)
Beginning set of hollow blocks:**
  Squares (4)
  Double squares (2)
  Half squares (4)
  Double half-squares (2)
  Ramps (2)
  Short boards (4)
  Long boards (2)

Cardboard blocks or blocks made
  from shoe boxes (48)
Milk cartons
Towels, bed spreads, old sheets,
  blankets
Boxes of various sizes
Wood scraps
Tubes
String
Rope
Steering wheels (2)
Small cars (24)
Small trucks (24)
Dollhouse families, various
  races/ethnicities (3 sets)
Small wooden trains (3)
Wooden train tracks (1 large set)
Street signs (1 set)
Large dinosaurs (1 set)
Farm animals (2 sets)
Zoo animals (2 sets)
Tinkertoys (1 large set)

* Many companies offer unit block sets with various shapes and numbers of blocks available. Unit blocks may also be ordered individually from the educational supply companies. In this guide, we recommend ordering unit blocks individually rather than in sets. The list given here may not have as many shape varieties as would be available in a prepackaged set, but it offers enough blocks of each shape so that several children can manipulate and build with blocks at the same time.

** Hollow blocks are usually ordered in sets. The contents of a typical set are listed here, but the number of each type of block will vary depending upon the set ordered.

Later Years

Additional unit blocks:
  Half units (10)
  Basic units (20)
  Double units (10)
  Quad units (4)
  Ramps (4)
  Unit arches (4)
  Half circles (2)
  Small half circles (4)
  Half Roman arches (4)
  Small buttresses (4)
  Quarter-circle arches (4)
  Half-circle arches (4)
  Crosses (2)
  Quarter circles (4)
  Gothic arches (2)
  Gothic arch doors (2)
  Cylinders (8)
  Double cylinders (4)
  Small triangles (4)
Additional set of hollow blocks:
  Squares (4)
  Double squares (2)
  Half squares (4)
  Double half-squares (2)
  Ramps (2)
  Short boards (4)
  Long boards (2)
Carpet pieces
Vinyl flooring scraps, sheet pieces
  or tiles
Barn
Garage
Lincoln Logs (1 large set)
Additional unit blocks, to be added
  over long term:
  Quad units (2)
  Ramps (2)
  Unit arches (2)
  Small half circles (2)
  Half Roman arches (2)

Small buttresses (2)
Quarter arches (4)
Gothic arches (2)
Gothic arch doors (2)
Cylinders (2)
Double cylinders (2)
Small triangles (16)
Double triangles (20)
Pillar units (10)
Double pillars (5)
Small roof boards (10)
Roof/floor boards (5)
Additional set of hollow blocks, to
  be added over long term:
Squares (8)
Double squares (4)
Half squares (8)
Double half-squares (4)
Ramps (4)
Short boards (8)
Long boards (4)
Large wooden trucks (4)
Large wooden cars (4)
Large wooden airplanes (2)
Sea life animals (2 sets)

---

*F*or more information on arranging and equipping the block area, see *Educating Young Children: Active Learning Practices for Preschool and Child Care Programs,* by Mary Hohmann and David P. Weikart, High/Scope Press, 1995, pp. 126–127.

4

The House Area

The house area is often a setting for children's pretending and dramatic play. Because preschoolers who are imitating older family members enjoy using full-sized objects, many of the materials found in the house area are "real" objects rather than toy replicas of these objects. For example, children can use adult-sized dishes and silverware, empty cracker boxes, and spice jars for pretend cooking experiences, and real baby bottles and bibs are available near the doll bed for baby-related play. Many house area materials can be acquired through donations from parents or by shopping at local discount or thrift stores.

In a High/Scope house area, a table (large enough to seat 10 children and an adult for small-group and snack times) replaces the traditional small table and chairs. (Usually, the other small group of children is seated at the art area table during these times.) To accommodate the larger table, the house area tends to take up a large part of the classroom. This area should be positioned close to the block area to allow children to combine props and toys from either area as they play.

The house area may also be positioned close to a water source so children can wash dishes or give toy babies their baths.

A shelving unit will be needed in this area for storing dishes and other props. One way to store the pots and pans is to hang them from hooks attached to the backs of the shelving units. An additional unit with hooks is needed for

Pegboard and hooks provide accessible storage for house area utensils. Outline labels indicate where each tool is stored.

hanging dress-up clothes, hats, purses, and bags. Hooks hung on the wall can be just as useful. If you are using a chest of drawers, be sure to put clear labels on the outside of each drawer. This way, the children know what's inside without having to open it.

House Area Equipment

First Year

Child-sized sink
Child-sized stove
Child-sized refrigerator
Shelving Units, 48"l x 30"h x 13"d (2)
Doll bed
Doll highchair

Table, large enough to seat 10
   children plus 1 adult
Chairs (11)
Mirror
Unit for hanging clothes

Later Years

Child-sized washer/dryer
Child-sized chest of drawers
Child-sized sofa

Child-sized easy chair
Child-sized rocking chair
Additional doll bed

House Area Materials

Note: Unless labeled otherwise, each item listed below is a full-sized "real" object rather than a toy replica.

First Year

Pots and pans (1 set)
Cooking utensils (1 set)
Tableware: forks, knives, spoons
   (12 place settings)
Plastic or Melamine plates, bowls, cups
   (12 place settings)
Spatulas (2 large, 2 small)
Mixing bowls (1 set)
Measuring cups (2 sets)
Measuring spoons (2 sets)
Potholders (2)
Sponges, dishcloths, towels
Plastic fruit (1 set)
Plastic vegetables (1 set)
Poker chips, may be used as money
   or food (1 set)
Bottle caps, may be used as money
   or food
Acorns, shells, small pine cones, and
   other natural materials
Food boxes, empty, for example,
   cracker or cereal boxes

Cans, cartons, jars, empty
Spice cans, empty
Telephones (2)
Telephone book
Computer keyboards, used (2)
Pads of paper (12)
Broom and dustpan
Props for pretend play (for example,
   barbershop, farm, fire station)
Dolls, various races/ethnicities (6)
Stuffed animals
Baby rattles (4)
Bibs (8)
Disposable diapers (1 box)
Baby blankets (8)
Baby clothes (a variety)
Baby bottles (8)
Dress-up clothes, shoes, and hats,
   both men's and women's
Sunglasses (12 pairs)
Purses (a variety)
Book bags

It's time to dress up for the dance.

Later Years

Small used appliances with cords cut off (toaster, coffee maker)
Kitchen timer
Ice-cube trays (2)
Hamburger press
Cake tin
Canister set
Sifter
Cloth napkins, place mats, tablecloth
Old clock

One-step stepladder
Plastic toolbox
Small vacuum cleaner
Luggage (1 set)
Cooler or ice chest
Desk
Additional props for pretend play
Additional dolls
Additional dress-up clothes
Sleeping bag

Children often combine materials from the house and block areas in their pretend play.

$\mathcal{F}$or more information on arranging and equipping the house area, see *Educating Young Children: Active Learning Practices for Preschool and Child Care Programs,* by Mary Hohmann and David P. Weikart, High/Scope Press, 1995, pp. 128–131.

The Toy Area

The toy area is equipped with small toys that children can build with, put together, take apart, and string. The toys in this area—such as dollhouses, people, and dinosaurs—often become part of children's pretend play. Natural materials, such as shells, rocks, pine cones, and nuts, are also placed in the toy area. These may be used by children for activities such as sorting, arranging in patterns, and weighing with a balance scale. Children playing in other areas of the room, such as the house area, may use items from the toy area as props in their dramatic play. Note that some of the toys listed below, such as the Duplo blocks, toy people, and vehicles, may be placed either in the block area or the toy area, depending on the interests of your group of children and the layout of your classroom. For example, in this book the

Small building toys can be located either in the toy or block areas.

Lincoln Logs and Tinkertoys are included in the block area list, but these materials could have been placed in the toy area.

The toy area should be a comfortable, carpeted space with ample room for the children to spread out the various toys. The shelving units serve both to define the area and to display the many toys available.

As in all of the areas in a High/Scope classroom, it is important to store the toys in this area so they are visible, for example, in clear plastic storage containers or open baskets. The task of choosing toys to play with is simpler for children when the toys are easy to see and clearly labeled.

The clothes this child needs to dress the small toy bears are visible in a clear container.

Toy Area Equipment

Shelving units, 48"l x 30"h x 13"d (2)

Puzzle storage chest,
  36"l x 24"h x 14"d

Toy Area Materials

First Year

Pegboard shape puzzle
Take-apart tube and marble game
  (50-piece set)
Marbles (set of 24)
Beads for stringing (set of 100)
  and laces (12)
Waffle blocks (set of 50)
Bristle Blocks (set of 100)
Duplo blocks (1 large set)
Duplo people (set of 15)
Duplo vehicles (set of 15)
Pegboards (12) and pegs (set of 300)
Teddy bear counters (set of 100)
Counting cubes (set of 100)

Unifix cubes (set of 100)
Magnetic marbles (set of 25)
  and wands (12)
Magnifying glass tripod
Balancing scale
Bead maze
Knobbed puzzles (a variety)
Jigsaw puzzles, 1–5 pieces
  (a variety)
Jigsaw puzzles, 6–11 pieces
  (a variety)
Jigsaw puzzles, 12 or more pieces
  (a variety)
Floor puzzles (a variety)

Later Years

Dollhouse
Dollhouse furniture, kitchen (1 set)
Dollhouse furniture, bathroom (1 set)
Dollhouse furniture, bedroom (1 set)
Dollhouse furniture, living room (1 set)
Dollhouse furniture, dining room
  (1 set)
Dollhouse people, various
  races/ethnicities (2 families)
Stacking rings or squares

Gears (set of 80)
Snap blocks (set of 60)
Flexiblocks (set of 300)
Interlocking pipes (set of 80)
Large plastic buttons (set of 150)
  and laces (12)
Plastic links (set of 500)
Magnet blocks (set of 50)
Additional puzzles
Additional floor puzzles

For more information on arranging and equipping the toy area, see *Educating Young Children: Active Learning Practices for Preschool and Child Care Programs,* by Mary Hohmann and David P. Weikart, High/Scope Press, 1995, pp. 136–137.

The Book Area

*T*he book area is a quiet place where children can go, alone or with friends, to snuggle up with a good book or a stuffed animal. To make it an enticing and welcoming place, the area is equipped with comfortable pillows, beanbag chairs, blankets, stuffed animals, and puppets. In many High/Scope classrooms, the book area also serves as the greeting time area, where children meet at the beginning of the day to explore books together and share announcements. Beginning the day in such a cozy place eases the transition from home to school.

An important consideration for the placement of the book area is to locate it away from noisy, high-traffic areas. Positioning the book area near a window provides a source of natural light for the children who are working there. Books may also be easily incorporated in other interest areas, if there isn't room in the classroom to accommodate a separate area for reading. Positioning the book shelf in the toy area or house area are two possible solutions when space is an issue. An example of this kind of arrangement is found in the sample classroom diagram on page 46.

For storing books, we recommend the type of bookrack that displays the book covers face-forward rather than the traditional bookshelf, which permits only the spines of the books to be seen. You will also need shelf space or baskets for storing puppets and stuffed animals. Although the lists in this book include puzzles only in the toy area, you may instead place them in the book area. In this case you will also need a puzzle rack.

A well-stocked and comfortable book area invites children to pause for a story at work time.

Book Area Equipment

First Year

Beanbag chairs (2)
Bookrack
Shelving unit, 48"l x 30"h x 13"d

Pillows (10)
Area rug

Later Years

Child-sized sofa

Child-sized rocking chair

Book Area Materials

First Year

A variety of the following types of books:

Caldecott Award books, such as *The Little House,* by Virginia Lee Burton

Classics, such as *Harry the Dirty Dog,* by Gene Zion

Predictable books, such as *The Very Hungry Caterpillar,* by Eric Carle

Self-concept books, such as *Peter's Chair,* by Ezra Jack Keats

Multicultural books, such as *Hats, Hats, Hats,* by Ann Morris

Special needs books, such as *The Handmade Alphabet,* by Laura Rankin

ABC books and counting books, such as *1,2,3,* by Tana Hoban

Books with real photographs, such as *Where Does It Go?,* by Margaret Miller

Special interest books relating to the interests of children in your class, such as *Cars and Trucks and Things That Go* by Richard Scarry, for children who are interested in vehicles.

Titles such as the above in big book format

Titles such as the above in board book format

Photo albums of children's field trips, classroom activities, children with their families, and so forth

Blankets
Flannel board
Flannel board materials
Stuffed animals (a variety)
Puppets (a variety)

Greeting time, in which children "read" a message board as they share daily announcements, is often held in the book area.

Later Years

Additional books
Additional flannel board materials
Magnet board
Magnet board magnets (a variety)

Magnetic letters (3 sets)
Tactile wood letter blocks (1 set)
Puppet stand

Children enjoy exploring books independently.

*F*or more information on arranging and equipping the book area, see *Educating Young Children: Active Learning Practices for Preschool and Child Care Programs,* by Mary Hohmann and David P. Weikart, High/Scope Press, 1995, pp. 138–139.

*I*n the computer area children work alone and cooperatively, playing games, writing stories, making patterns, drawing pictures, and solving problems that arise as they work. When establishing a computer area, take care to select computer programs that are appropriate for young children. If the programs you choose are appropriate, the computer area will be a popular area for the children in your class.

Developmentally appropriate, high-quality software holds children's attention.

As you do for other classroom areas, plan your computer area to avoid child conflicts over the use of the equipment. If your budget permits, provide several computers per classroom. Position them close to one another with two chairs at each, to encourage conversation and cooperative problem solving. Placing the computer area in a corner of the room or against the wall will keep cords and plugs away from child traffic.

The monitors, keyboards, and printers will all stay on the computer station, so there are very few materials to store. Many of the programs can be put on the computer's hard drive. Any program disks used by the children may need to be kept in a storage box. In addition, keep a backup disk for each of these programs in a location not accessible to the children.

Arrange the computer area to allow children to work cooperatively at the computers.

Computer Area Equipment

First Year

Computer stations (3)
Windows or Macintosh computers (3)
  Windows specifications—

  Processor: 486SX or above @33MHZ or faster

  RAM: 8MB or greater (4MB is sufficient for some programs)

  Monitor: SVGA color 512K video RAM or greater (256 or more colors)

  Sound: Sound Blaster or compatible w/speakers (16 bit)

  Hard Drive: 350MB or greater

  CD-ROM: Double speed or greater

  System: DOS 5.0 or higher and Windows 3.1 or Windows 95

Macintosh specifications—

  Processor: 68040 or above @33MHZ or faster or PowerPC

  RAM: 8MB or greater (4MB is sufficient for some programs)

  Monitor: 256 or more colors

  Sound: yes (card and speakers may be built in)

  Hard Drive: 340MB or greater

  CD-ROM: Double speed or faster (may be built in)

  System: 7 or higher

Dot matrix or ink jet printer, color if possible, with automatic print-sharing switch

Chairs (6)

Later Years

Additional computers and stations

Additional chairs

Computer Area Materials

First Year

Printer paper
Early childhood computer programs (a variety) for example:
  Bailey's Book House (Edmark)
  Just Grandma and Me (Broderbund)

Kid Pix 2 (Broderbund)
Millie's Math House (Edmark)
Sammy's Science House (Edmark)
Thinkin' Things Collection 1 (Edmark)
The Tortoise & the Hare (Broderbund)

Later Years

Additional computer programs

---

*F*or more information on arranging and equipping the computer area, see *Educating Young Children: Active Learning Practices for Preschool and Child Care Programs,* by Mary Hohmann and David P. Weikart, High/Scope Press, 1995, pp. 142–143, and *High/Scope Buyer's Guide to Children's Software,* by Charles Hohmann, Barbara Carmody, and Chica McCabe-Branz, High/Scope Press, 1995.

---

*I*n the movement and music area, children experiment with simple instruments, such as xylophones, tambourines, maracas, and triangles. They also enjoy making up games with the scarves, streamers, and bean bags that are found there. An inviting movement and music area includes a tape recorder and tapes, so children can listen to, move with, and dance to music.

This area tends to be noisy, so consider positioning it next to the house or block area. It may also be placed near the large-group gathering place, allowing easy access to the instruments and other movement props during large-group time. Once again, when space is an issue, the movement and music materials can easily be integrated into other areas, such as the block area.

Children use scarves from the movement and music area for a variety of movement experiences and may also incorporate them into their pretend play with dolls.

These children are inventing their own music.

Storing the musical instruments on one shelf and the movement materials on another is one way of displaying the items in this area. An equally effective way to display the instruments is to hang them on pegboard hooks. If you choose this method, trace outlines of the instruments on the pegboard so children know where to hang each one.

Movement and Music Area Equipment

First Year

Shelving unit, 48"l x 30"h x 13"d

Later Years

Shelving unit, 48"l x 30"h x 13"d

Musical instruments and movement materials are placed next to a large open space so there is plenty of room for children to move around.

Movement and Music Area Materials

First Year

Cassette tape player or CD player
Instrumental music tapes
  (a variety, including selections from
  High/Scope's *Rhythmically
  Moving* series of recordings)
Vocal music tapes (a variety)
Story tapes (a variety)
Blank tapes for children's use
Beanbags (24)
Hula hoops (24)
Scarves (24)

Plastic circles for moving on or
  around, 8"diameter (24)
Rhythm sticks (24 pairs)
Triangles (2)
Wrist bells (24)
Sand blocks (12)
Maracas (1 pair)
Instruments from cultures
  of children in program
Wooden xylophones (2)
Tambourines (6)
Tom-tom drums (6)

Later Years

Ribbon wands (24)
Streamers (24)
Finger cymbals (4 pairs)
Brass cymbals (2 pairs)

Handle castanets (6)
Tone blocks and mallets (6)
Balance beam (1 set)

---

*F*or more information on arranging and equipping the music and movement area, see *Educating Young Children: Active Learning Practices for Preschool and Child Care Programs,* by Mary Hohmann and David P. Weikart, High/Scope Press, 1995, p. 141.

The Sand and Water Area 9

*T*he sand and water area is a place where children, working alone or together, can experience fluids, granular materials, and other consumable materials such as water, snow, sand, and sawdust. Dried beans, colored rice, cereal, and used coffee grounds may also be used if staff of your program feel comfortable with children using food for play. While pouring, dumping, mixing, filling, and emptying these materials, children are learning space and number concepts and language. Children also enjoy pretending in this area—baking birthday cakes with the rice, constructing roads in the wet sand, or making castles and swimming pools with sand and water.

Locating the sand and water area near the classroom's water source makes it convenient to fill and empty the water table and clean up sandy toys and spilled sand. Also desirable is tile or vinyl flooring, which makes cleanup easier when water or sand has been spilled on the floor. Since both the art area and sand and water area need a water source and easily cleaned flooring, it makes sense to locate the sand and water area near or within the art area. Store smocks to keep children's clothes clean and dry so they are convenient to both these areas.

Choose shelves and storage containers for this area that allow materials to drain and dry, for example, rust-proof wire shelving and plastic, open-weave baskets. Stackable plastic storage crates can be substituted for traditional shelving units. When mounted to the wall, these can be very sturdy. Label the storage containers and shelves and place them at the children's level to foster children's independence and make cleanup go more smoothly.

Expect both social and solitary play at the sand and water area.

Sand and Water Area Equipment

First Year

Sand or water table with lid	Shelving unit that allows sand toys to drain, 48"l x 30"h x 13"d

Later Years

Additional sand or water table with lid (may be used outside if space is not available indoors) Additional shelving unit (choose one that allows sand toys to drain)	Replacement liner for water table (may be necessary after about 10 years' use)

Sand and Water Area Materials

First Year

Sand Water Food coloring (for coloring water) Dishwashing liquid (for bubbles) Shovels (12) Buckets (12) Sifters (6) Strainers (6) Plastic cars, small (12) Plastic trucks (12) Plastic boats (12)	Funnels (12) Measuring cups (3 sets) Measuring spoons (3 sets) Shells Turkey basters (12) Squeeze bottles (12) Sponges (a variety) Vinyl smocks (shared with art area) Dustpan and broom Towels

Later Years

Dried beans, peas, corn, colored rice, used coffee grounds (if program staff feel comfortable using food for play) Sawdust Wood shavings	Water wheels (4) Sand combs (12) Siphons and pumps (4) Baby dolls, washable (2)

To offer a different kind of filling and emptying experience, try filling the table with dry beans.

*F*or more information on arranging and equipping the sand and water area, see *Educating Young Children: Active Learning Practices for Preschool and Child Care Programs,* by Mary Hohmann and David P. Weikart, High/Scope Press, 1995, pp. 124–125.

In the woodworking area, children hammer, saw, and fasten nuts and bolts together, using "real" construction materials and tools. Working with tools that they have seen adults using is an exciting experience for children. Children working in this area often make play props—for example, a telephone to use in the house area or an airplane to use after building an airport in the block area.

The woodworking area tends to be a noisy area because of the pounding and sawing. Therefore, it makes sense to position this area near other noisy areas, such as the block area or music and movement area. Children often use art materials, such as paint, markers, tape, or glue, to decorate creations made in the woodworking area, so positioning this area next to the art area also has advantages. Locating the woodworking area outdoors so children can use it at outside time is another solution that works well for many programs. If space is an issue, consider locating some of the materials normally found in the woodworking area elsewhere in the classroom. For example, materials such as blocks of wood, Styrofoam pieces, glue, wire, and paint can go

When safety equipment is always provided, children learn to associate it with the fun of using construction tools.

in the art area, and real nuts and bolts make an excellent addition to the toy area.

We recommend using low shelves to separate the woodworking area from the flow of classroom traffic. The low shelves also provide space for storing the materials. Outlines or pictures of the various tools can serve as labels. Sample pieces of the smaller hardware can also be used as labels.

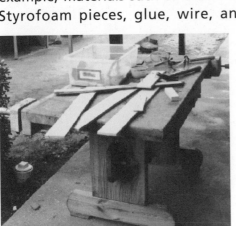

If there is no room for a woodworking area indoors, construction materials may be brought outdoors in good weather.

Woodworking Area Equipment

Workbench

Shelving unit, 48"l x 30"h x 13"d

Woodworking Area Materials

Safety goggles (12 pairs)
Styrofoam blocks
Golf tees (set of 100)
Lightweight hammers (6)
Assorted wood pieces*
Nails, various sizes
  (enough to fill a 38-oz. can)
Saws (6)

Screwdrivers (6)
Screws, various sizes
  (enough to fill a 38-oz. can)
Wire (5 packages)
Pliers (6 pairs)
Hand drills (2)
Clamps (6)
Sandpaper

For more information on arranging and equipping the woodworking area, see *Educating Young Children: Active Learning Practices for Preschool and Child Care Programs,* by Mary Hohmann and David P. Weikart, High/Scope Press, 1995, p. 140.

---

* Soft pine is easiest for children to hammer and saw.

*I*n the outdoor area children enjoy swinging, running, climbing, balancing, digging, pedaling, throwing, and catching. Just as they do in the classroom, they are exploring their surroundings. The outdoor area is a perfect space for painting, playing in water, and engaging in other messy activities. It is also a space where noise levels are not a concern—rhythm instruments may not seem so noisy when they're taken outside to be played.

The outdoor area should be close or adjacent to the center and enclosed by a fence for safety. The larger the area, the more options teachers will have in planning outside time, and the more space the children will have to explore. Children need paved pathways for riding toys, open areas for swings, areas for climbing structures surfaced with wood chips or pea gravel, grassy areas with hills for rolling and running, and areas of dirt or sand for digging.

It's fun to take bubble-making materials outdoors on a sunny day.

When considering materials and equipment for children's use outdoors, be sure to include plenty of loose materials to support children's pretending, building, digging, filling and emptying, and outdoor artwork. For ideas for loose materials that may be used outside, refer to the lists for the house, art, sand and water, and movement and music areas. You will also want to include traditional playground equipment, such as climbing structures, swings, riding toys, and balls. Remember that outdoor play can be quiet as well as boisterous, and that children need materials that allow them to use their imaginations as well as their bodies.

We recommend a storage shed for the loose materials and toys used outside, but if one is not available, provide baskets for carrying loose materials inside to keep them from getting ruined by the elements. If a storage shed is available, consider adding shelves and labeling them just as you would in the classroom.

Remember to consider the social aspects of swinging as you choose swings for the playground.

Outdoor Equipment

First Year

Swings (3)   Large sandbox
Climber (with options for expansion)   Storage shed for outside equipment
Slide (part of climber)

Later Years

Tire swing   Tubs with soil or garden
Balance beam   Window boxes
Tree house   Expanded climber
Water table   Low canvas or net hammock
Low-hung basketball hoop

Outdoor Materials

First Year

Tricycles (6)
Wagons (2)
Balls (large and small) (6)
Child-sized shovels and rakes (12)
Sifters (6)
Strainers (6)

Funnels (12)
Plastic squeeze bottles (12)
Large sponges (12)
Vinyl smocks (12)
Refrigerator boxes (staples removed)
Old tires

Later Years

Sleds or, in warm climates,
   additional wagons (6)
Hanging easels (6)
Gardening tools: shovels, rakes,
   buckets (6 each)
Seeds, bulbs, flowers, plants
Watering cans (6)
Garden Hose
Scooters (2)
Beanbags (24)

Paint buckets and house-painting
   brushes (12)
White paper, 36" wide
   (2 rolls, each 1000')
Parachute
Wheelbarrow
Strollers (2)
Inner tubes (2)
Boards of varying lengths
Old sheets, blankets

If you have a storage shed for the loose materials children use outdoors, you don't have to carry as many materials in and out of the center daily.

*F*or more information on arranging and equipping the outdoor area, see *Educating Young Children: Active Learning Practices for Preschool and Child Care Programs,* by Mary Hohmann and David P. Weikart, High/Scope Press, 1995, pp. 144–145; *Supporting Young Learners,* edited by Nancy A. Brickman and Lynn S. Taylor, High/Scope Press, 1991, pp. 167–173; *Supporting Young Learners 2,* edited by Nancy A. Brickman, High/Scope Press, 1995, pp. 119–126; and *The Early Childhood Playground: An Outdoor Classroom,* by Steen Esbensen, High/Scope Press, 1987.

*I*n addition to the materials in the interest areas, the following materials and equipment are recommended for active learning preschool programs. This list includes both materials for general use and materials for adult use only.

Miscellaneous Classroom Equipment and Materials

Cubbies for personal belongings, 48"l x 36"h x 14"d (1 set)

Coat hooks (20)

Carpeting or rugs in all areas except art area

Large-group rug

Plastic floor mats to go under easel and water table (4)

Bulletin boards for parent board and children's artwork (4)

Refrigerator

Wipe-off board

Medium-sized baskets for snacks (4)

Plastic cups, heavy-duty (24)

Plastic pitchers (4)

Metal forks, knives, spoons (24 of each)

Plates and bowls (24)

Paper napkins, as needed

Buckets (2)

Sponges (20)

1 cassette player/CD player for adults' use at large-group time

File cabinet for student files

Miscellaneous office supplies

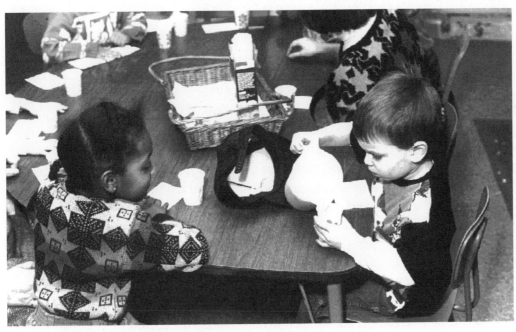

Snack time supplies and utensils are part of the classroom's miscellaneous equipment. Choose small pitchers that are easily handled by children.

Teacher Resources

It is essential for teachers to have a library of resource books to refer to when they have questions or concerns about various topics. Listed below are books and videos from High/Scope Press that provide information on such topics as active learning, the daily routine, parent involvement, the learning environment, activities you can share with the children you teach, and music and movement ideas.

Ongoing teacher training is another important tool for professional development. High/Scope offers training year-round both at its headquarters in Ypsilanti, Michigan, and in areas near you. High/Scope training opportunities range from one- and two-day introductory workshops to longer term certification programs for lead teachers and teacher-trainers. Workshops and courses are available on many topics. For example, a few of High/Scope's most popular workshops are those on adult-child interactions, setting up the learning environment, and using the High/Scope Child Observation Record (COR), High/Scope's child assessment tool. Taking advantage of High/Scope's teacher-training opportunities is an excellent way to gain a better understanding of how to implement a high-quality early childhood program. A complete list of High/Scope books, videos, and training opportunities may be obtained by calling 1-800-40-PRESS (FAX 1-800-442-4FAX), or visit our web site at www.highscope.org to obtain the complete High/Scope Press Catalog as well as program and training information. Following is a list of essential High/Scope references for teachers.

High/Scope Books, Assessment Tools, Recorded Music, Videos

First Year

✔ **Educating Young Children: Active Learning Practices for Preschool and Child Care Programs.** Written for early childhood practitioners and students, this manual presents essential strategies adults can use to make active learning a reality in their programs. The book describes key components of the adult's role, including planning the physical setting, establishing a consistent daily routine, creating a positive social climate, and using High/Scope's 58 "key experiences" to understand and support young children. Other topics include family involvement, daily team planning, creating interest areas, choosing appropriate materials, the plan-do-review process, small- and large-group times. This comprehensive guide offers numerous anecdotes, photographs, illustrations, real-life scenarios, and practical suggestions for adults. It is based on High/Scope research findings and 30 years of practical experience. *M. Hohmann & D. P. Weikart. Soft cover, lavishly illustrated, 560 pages, 1995, $39.95.*

✔ **High/Scope Extensions: Newsletter of the High/Scope Curriculum.** Learn about the High/Scope approach from High/Scope consultants and trainers. This newsletter is packed with practical tips, suggestions, and updated information to help you understand and implement the High/Scope Curriculum or train others to do so. Special features include "Classroom Hints," "Ask Us," "Network News," "Trainer-to-Trainer," and "Computer Learning." *N. Brickman, Editor. Eight pages per issue, 6 issues per year, $30.95 annually.*

✔ **Supporting Young Learners 1: Ideas for Preschool and Day Care Providers.** This collection of articles from the *High/Scope Extensions* newsletter provides practical answers to the day-to-day questions that arise in early childhood programs. *N. Brickman & L. Taylor, Editors. Soft cover, 314 pages, 1991, $25.95.*

✔ **Supporting Young Learners 2: Ideas for Child Care Providers and Teachers.** This second collection of articles from the *High/Scope Extensions* newsletter is packed with practical strategies and tips for making an active learning program the best

The classroom above provides large divided cubbies both for children's possessions and their outerwear, while High/Scope's demonstration classroom meets the same needs with coat hooks and separate cubbies (below).

it can be. It contains over 50 articles that have been updated to reflect the latest thinking on the High/Scope Curriculum. *N. Brickman, Editor. Soft cover, many photos, 328 pages, 1996, $25.95.*

✔ **Program Implementation Profile: Administration Manual.** The Program Implementation Profile (PIP) is an ideal evaluation tool for all early childhood settings. This manual helps you rate your program site according to physical environment, daily routine, adult-child interaction, and adult-adult interaction. The PIP can also be used for training and for pinpointing specific areas needing improvement. The manual includes the evaluation instrument. *Soft cover, 37 pages, 1989, $11.95.*

✔ **High/Scope ReSource: A Magazine for Educators.** *ReSource* is a guide to the activities, products, and services of the High/Scope Foundation. This free publication includes useful articles, important training opportunities, and a complete catalog of High/Scope publications and training opportunities. *L. Taylor, editor, 3 issues per year.*

✔ ***The Early Childhood Playground: An Outdoor Classroom.*** Learn about safe, effective alternatives to commonly used playground equipment and landscaping. *S. B. Esbensen. Soft cover, 48 pages, 1987, $10.95.*

✔ ***Young Children and Computers.*** This book explains how to get started using computers in preschool and kindergarten, what equipment and software are needed, and how computer activities fit into the daily routine. *C. Hohmann. Soft cover, 128 pages, 1990, $15.95.*

✔ ***High/Scope Buyer's Guide to Children's Software, 11th Edition.*** High/Scope's latest survey of computer programs for children aged 3–7 contains in-depth reviews of 48 software programs and descriptions and ratings of over 500 more. Find out which software programs are best and why. The guide also includes award-winning programs, a glossary, and a national directory of software producers. *C. Hohmann, B. Carmody, & C. McCabe-Branz. Soft cover, 196 pages, 1995.*

✔ ***Movement Plus Music: Activities for Children Ages 3 to 7.*** This book outlines movement activities for young children and gives suggestions for synchronizing the activities to music. The author focuses on moving in coordinated ways, following directions, feeling and expressing the beat, and moving creatively. *P. S. Weikart. Soft cover, 40 pages, 1989, $10.95.*

Later Years

✔ ***The Teacher's Idea Book 1: Daily Planning Around the Key Experiences.*** Make each part of the daily routine a useful and focused learning experience for preschoolers and kindergartners with the practical, creative suggestions in this handbook. Packed with specific ideas for each part of the daily routine, this book includes suggestions for materials, questioning techniques, and small- and large-group activities. *M. Graves. Soft cover, 87 pages, 1989, $19.95.*

✔ ***The Teacher's Idea Book 2: Planning Around Children's Interests.*** This second book in High/Scope's popular series is packed with practical teaching strategies and actual classroom examples of teacher-child interactions. All new, up-to-date, and fun for all, the ideas draw on children's interests as a rich resource for curriculum planning. *M. Graves. Soft cover, photos, 171 pages, 1996, $25.95.*

✔ ***Getting Involved: Workshops for Parents.*** This book presents a dynamic series of one-hour workshops for teachers to present to parents of young children. The workshops allow parents to participate in activities they can use at home with their children. The book can be an essential tool for building strong parent involvement in children's learning. *E. Frede. Soft cover, 306 pages, 1984, $15.95.*

✔ **Round the Circle: Key Experiences in Movement for Children.** This book offers age-appropriate movement activities and presents important key experiences. The author explains the important learning opportunities inherent in movement experiences. *P. S. Weikart. Soft cover, 125 pages, 1987, $19.95.*

✔ **Movement Plus Rhymes, Songs, & Singing Games.** This is a collection of engaging, age-appropriate movement activities for children that supplement those described in *Round the Circle.* Use them during circle time, small-group time, or transitions. *P. S. Weikart et al. Soft cover, 104 pages, 1988, $14.95.*

✔ **Movement in Steady Beat.** This manual presents a collection of unique rhymes and action songs for children aged 3 to 7. The activities focus on the movement key experience *feeling and expressing beat. P. S. Weikart. Soft cover, 96 pages, 1990, $14.95.*

✔ **High/Scope Child Observation Record (COR) for Ages 2½–6.** The COR, High/Scope's child assessment instrument, provides an observational assessment system that teachers use during normal classroom activities. This developmentally appropriate instrument is an alternative to test-based assessment systems. The instrument is also available in software versions for IBM and compatibles or Macintosh computers. The High/Scope Child Observation Record Kit includes all the materials needed for a full year of assessment for a classroom of 25 children. *Boxed COR Kit: Manual, 25 Assessment Booklets, 4 sets Anecdotal Notecards, 50 Parent Report Forms, Poster, $90.95; COR-PC Kit, $149.95; COR-Mac Kit, $149.95*

✔ **Adult-Child Interactions: Forming Partnerships With Children.** This video shows teachers at High/Scope's Demonstration Preschool in Ypsilanti, Michigan, interacting as partners with children throughout the daily routine. Part 1 introduces interaction strategies, demonstrates their use in two work time scenes, and includes a teacher commentary on each scene. Part 2 contains additional classroom scenes presented without commentary to encourage viewer analysis and discussion. *Video guide included. Color video, 60 min., 1996, $50.95—purchase, $10—rental.*

✔ **Drawing and Painting: Ways to Support Young Artists.** Gather ideas for creative art activities in your classroom from Greek educator and artist Eli Trimis, who is featured in this video program. *Video guide included. Color slides transferred to video, 34 min., 1996, $50.95—purchase, $10—rental.*

✔ **Setting Up the Learning Environment.** How to set up and equip play and work spaces that will engage children in active learning is the topic of this video. *Color video, 20 min., 1992, $30.95—purchase, $10.00—rental.*

✔ **The High/Scope Curriculum: The Daily Routine.** Shot entirely at High/Scope's Demonstration Preschool, this informative video highlights the rationale for each segment of the daily routine. *Color video, 17 min., 1990, $30.95—purchase, $10—rental.*

✔ **Supporting Children's Active Learning: Teaching Strategies for Diverse Settings.** This video illustrates a range of teaching techniques you can adopt to facilitate children's active learning. *Color video, 13 min., 1989, $30.95—purchase, $10—rental.*

✔ **The High/Scope Curriculum: The Plan-Do-Review Process.** This video illustrates the central element of the High/Scope daily routine, the plan-do-review process. This process is depicted in preschool, child care, and special needs settings. *Color video, 20 min., 1989, $30.95—purchase, $10—rental.*

✔ **Visiting High/Scope's Demonstration Preschool: How Adults Support Children at Planning Time.** This video is packed with tips and strategies for making the most of planning time experiences and interactions. *Color video, 1997, $19.95.*

✔ **Visiting High/Scope's Demonstration Preschool: How Adults Support Children at Work Time.** This video depicts actual work time situations and a variety of strategies for supporting children's initiatives at work time. *Color video, 1997, $19.95.*

✔ **Visiting High/Scope's Demonstration Preschool: How Adults Support Children at Recall Time.** Using actual classroom scenes as illustrations, this video shows how adults can encourage children to talk about and reflect on their experiences at work time. *Color video, 1997, $19.95.*

✔ **Computer Learning for Young Children.** This video leads you through each step of setting up computers in the classroom. *Color video, 13 min., 1989, $30.95—purchase, $10—rental.*

✔ **Small-Group Time Video Series.**

1. Counting With Bears. Strategies for planning small-group time are outlined. *Color video, 13 min., $30.95—purchase, $10—rental*

2. Plan-Do-Review With Found Materials. A teacher plans, then carries out her plan and evaluates the outcome with another teacher. *Color video, 25 min., $30.95—purchase, $10—rental.*

3. Working With Staplers. Child management issues are highlighted as children experiment with staplers. *Color video, 12 min., $30.95—purchase, $10—rental.*

4. Representing With Sticks and Balls. This program demonstrates how to listen to children and elaborate on their ideas. *Color video, 14 min., $30.95—purchase, $10—rental.*

5. Exploring With Paint & Corks. The teacher involves children in planning and decision making as they work with small-group materials. *Color video, 12 min., $30.95—purchase, $10—rental.*

✔ **Rhythmically Moving 1–9.** This instrumental music series includes a variety of folk melodies from the U.S. and around the world, including many familiar favorites as well as less well-known tunes. All selections have a clear, steady beat and are ideal for classroom music and movement experiences. *P. S. Weikart, creative director. Cassettes, CDs, or 33⅓ RPM records. Each record or cassette, $10.95; each CD, $15.*

€ach High/Scope learning environment is unique because each teaching team implements High/Scope's room arrangement principles in a different way. Teams must consider a wide range of factors as they design their settings. These variables include both the fixed physical characteristics of the classroom or center and the interests and needs of the group of children who are enrolled in the program in a given year. In the pages that follow we present four sample "maps" of High/Scope preschool classrooms that illustrate some of the variations we can expect among High/Scope settings. The description given with each diagram explains some of the factors considered in planning each room arrangement.

High/Scope room arrangement principles are the same for all settings but these principles are applied in varied ways. Above is the spacious art area in the High/Scope Demonstration Classroom. Below, in a Mexican preschool, found materials used in art projects are neatly stacked on wooden crates. Below left, in a Georgia preschool, art materials are brought outside on a sunny day.

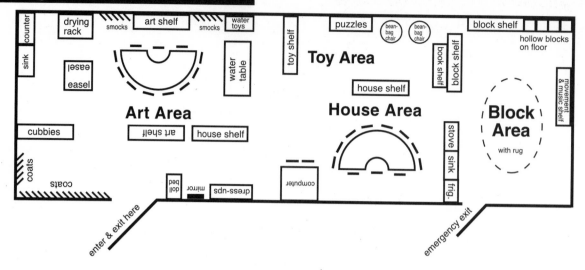

Room Arrangements 1A and 1B

In the first arrangement, you will notice that the size of the classroom is very small. The dimensions, 40' x 13', are typical of the trailers that are commonly used for classrooms. One of the biggest challenges in a classroom of this size is, of course, dealing with limited space.

In arranging a small classroom, you may want to consider including only the four basic interest areas (house area, block area, art area, and toy area), as shown in the first illustration. Having only these basic areas doesn't mean that you must eliminate the materials that would traditionally be found in other areas, such as books, instruments, computers, or hammers. Some of these materials can often be incorporated in the basic areas. For example, in Room Arrangement 1A, you will see that a shelf with music and movement materials was placed in the block area. The teaching team knew that children would need ample space to move with movement materials like beanbags and scarves. The teachers also decided that instruments, like blocks, tend to be noisy, so placing the music and movement shelf in the block area made sense to them. Similarly, rather than having separate toy and book areas, the classroom teachers saw that the children in the toy area were mostly using puzzles, stringing beads, and playing with the dollhouse, and their play was very calm. Because the children's play in that area was so quiet, the teachers felt that putting the books and beanbag chairs in the toy area was a logical move. You will also see that the classroom illustrated in 1A has only one computer so the teachers decided to place it in the house area, rather than set up a separate computer area.

The second illustration, 1B, shows the same classroom, designed by the same teachers, with some slight differences in the arrangement because of a new school year and a new group of children. With this second group of children, the teachers had noticed that the children playing in the toy area were much more rambunctious than the children of the year before had been in that area. Instead of stringing beads and putting together puzzles, the children were using the materials to make fighter planes and action figures

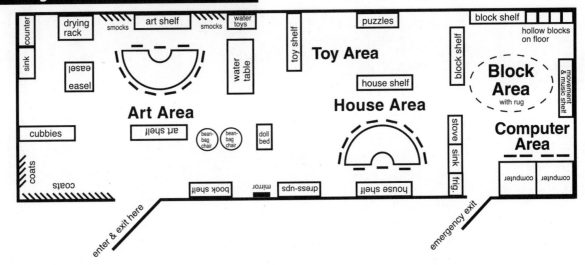

and their play was louder and more active. The teachers also observed that the books in this area weren't being used. They therefore decided to move the books and beanbag chairs to the house area, hoping that the quieter setting would encourage more reading. After doing this, the teachers observed children reading books to their "babies" and using the beanbag chairs as beds for their "sick children." Another change that was made in the classroom was the addition of a computer station. Because of this added equipment the teachers felt it necessary to remove the computer from the house area and create a separate computer area.

Room Arrangement 2

The second design (see next page) is the classroom at the High/Scope Demonstration Preschool in Ypsilanti, Michigan. At 53' x 21' this room is larger than the first, but still long and narrow. The room has a tile floor near the sink and the bathroom, while the rest of the room (aside from the area by the entryway) is carpeted. Because art activities are messy, it made sense to the teachers to locate the art area in the space that has the tile floor and the sink. This makes cleanup convenient and easy. For similar reasons the water table was also placed on the tile floor. You will notice that the shelf with the movement materials was placed in the block area, so the children would have plenty of room to move. The teachers put the shelf with the musical instruments in the toy area, because they had observed some of the children exploring the sounds made by toy area materials, for example, putting acorns in plastic containers and shaking them like maracas. They felt that putting real instruments in this area was a way of building on children's interest in creating sounds. They agreed that they would watch the children to see if their interest in the music and movement materials increased. If this occurred, they would then discuss the possibility of setting up a separate music and movement area. The teachers also included a woodworking area in this classroom. They decided to add the woodworking area after seeing several children glueing wood pieces together and then painting their new creations in the art area.

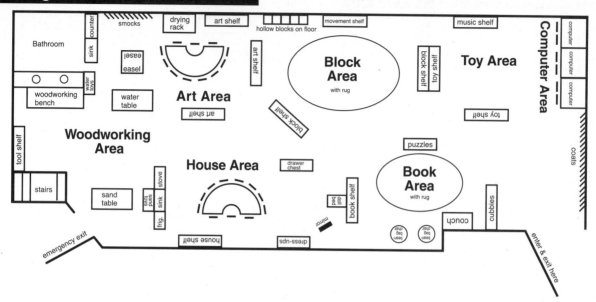

As was mentioned before, the book area usually doubles as the greeting time place at the beginning of the day. In designing this room, the teachers agreed to place that area near the door so children can see their parents leave and so the teacher there can easily see who is arriving. There is also a window in that area, and children enjoy waving to their friends as they come to school and waving goodbye to their parents as they leave.

Room Arrangement 3

The last arrangement (see next page) is an example of a large and very spacious room, approximately 36' x 30' (in the deepest part of the room). Because space was ample, the teachers decided to divide the house area into three sections. Notice that the teachers arranged the kitchen materials in one part of the house area, the couch and chair in another part of the area, and dress-up clothes, doll bed, and baby materials in still another part of the area. In so doing, the teachers created spaces that could represent a kitchen, living room, and bedroom. The teachers observed that the children in their classroom were interested in listening to music and marching with the instruments, so they designated an area of the room as the music and movement area. Positioning that area near the block area gave children plenty of room to move with movement materials and instruments. During the year, the teachers noticed their children positioning the large hollow blocks on the floor, making paths to march on with their instruments.

While it is convenient to have a classroom that is spacious, it is possible to have a room that is too large. In these cases, children and teachers may feel overwhelmed by the large space. In such a room, it may be necessary to use some of the classroom space for teacher storage, using shelving units to demarcate that area, and making the area of the classroom that the children will use smaller.

All teachers have unique challenges to face when designing their classrooms, whether their rooms are large or small. When designing all

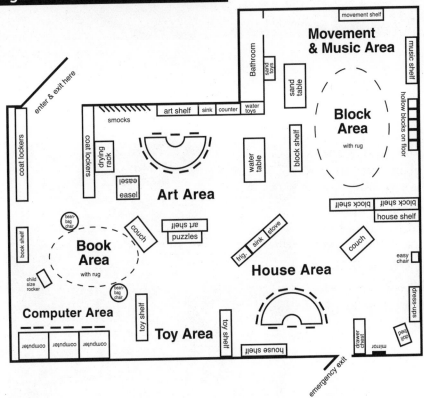

three of the room arrangements shown, the teaching teams were aware of the changing interests and needs of their groups of children. They were also aware of the need to modify their room arrangements by periodically adding new materials. As you arrange or rearrange your own preschool classroom or center, you may wish to make a diagram of your classroom similar to the room arrangements shown here. This will help you experiment with various layouts before you move all of your equipment.

In offering you these sample room arrangements, lists of suggested equipment and materials, and basic guidelines for arranging your classroom, this book is intended to be a helpful source of room arrangement ideas for you and other preschool teachers. If you have additional questions or concerns regarding the physical learning environment or other aspects of the High/Scope Curriculum, we encourage you to utilize the list of references given earlier and to take advantage of the unique training opportunities that High/Scope offers.

We understand that setting up an active learning environment can be a challenging, time-consuming task. Nevertheless, the learning environment is an essential element of the High/Scope Curriculum, and taking the time to develop, modify, and make additions to it is a necessary step for providing an effective program. It is our hope that the suggestions in this book will give you many ideas for creating an active learning environment that is interesting, exciting, and stimulating for the children that you teach!

*N*ancy Vogel teaches at the High/Scope Demonstration Preschool in Ypsilanti, Michigan and is a certified High/Scope preschool trainer. She has taught in various early childhood settings, including state-funded preschools, early childhood special education programs, and kindergarten programs. She holds a B.S. degree in Early Childhood Education from Bradley University, Peoria, Illinois.